A to

PEACE ON EARTH

CHRISTMAS IS...

BY GAIL GIBBONS

Holiday House / *New York*

Copyright © 2001 by Gail Gibbons

All rights reserved

Printed in the United States of America

www.holidayhouse.com

First Edition

Library of Congress Cataloging-in-Publication Data

Gibbons, Gail.

Christmas Is . . . / Gail Gibbons.—1st ed.

p. cm.

ISBN 0-8234-1582-1 (hardcover)

1. Christmas trees—Juvenile literature.

2. Christmas—Juvenile literature.

[1. Christmas trees.   2. Christmas.]

I. Title.

GT4989. G53 2001

394.2663-dc21   00-054686

CHRISTMAS IS…THE CHRIST CHILD.

Christmas celebrates the birth of Jesus Christ.
It is on December 25th.

Many years ago in the town of Bethlehem, the baby Jesus was born in a stable. His parents, Mary and Joseph, were traveling and could not find shelter at the inn, so they placed him in a manger.

On that night an angel told three shepherds of the the birth of Christ the Lord. They traveled to Bethlehem to find him.

In the dark night sky, a bright star appeared over Bethlehem. Three wise men followed it to the stable. They brought the Christ child gifts.

The shepherds and the wise men worshiped the Christ child. They were joyful and believed he was the Son of God, who would bring peace and love to the world.

CHRISTMAS HAS MANY SYMBOLS.
CHRISTMAS IS…ANGELS.

Hark! The herald angels sing!

Angels announced the coming of the Christ child.

CHRISTMAS IS…THE CRÈCHE.

A crèche (cresh) is a display of the manger scene at the birth of the Christ child.

CHRISTMAS IS...SAINT NICHOLAS

Saint Nicholas lived a long time ago. He loved giving gifts and helping people.

AND SANTA CLAUS.

Over time, he became known as Santa Claus.

It is said that Saint Nicholas threw three bags of gold down a chimney where three poor girls lived. One of the bags landed in a stocking hung by the chimney to dry.

Maybe that is why nowadays stockings are hung for Santa to fill, and why some people think Santa slides down chimneys.

CHRISTMAS IS...SANTA'S REINDEER, TOO.

Many people say Santa Claus jumps into his sleigh on Christmas Eve to deliver gifts. His reindeer pull him through the starry sky.

CHRISTMAS IS...THE CHRISTMAS TREE.

A Christmas tree is an evergreen. It stays green year-round.

Some people pick out a tree and bring it home to decorate.

CHRISTMAS IS...CHRISTMAS LIGHTS.

Many people decorate their Christmas trees with lights. The lights look like heavenly stars. The star on top of the tree represents the bright star that appeared over Bethlehem.

Some people put candles in their windows and decorate their homes with lights.

The Christmas lights are to remind people of the light the Christ child brought into the world when he was born.

CHRISTMAS IS...CHRISTMAS ORNAMENTS.

Many people decorate their Christmas trees with ornaments.

CHRISTMAS IS... HOLLY, WREATHS, MISTLETOE,

HOLLY

WREATH

MISTLETOE

Christmas greens and flowers add to the joyous atmosphere.

AND POINSETTIAS, TOO.

The poinsettia is the most popular flower at Christmastime. In Central America it is called the Flower of the Holy Night.

CHRISTMAS IS...CHRISTMAS CARDS.

People remember family and friends, and send cards wishing them joy.

CHRISTMAS IS...GIFT GIVING.

The three wise men brought gifts to the Christ child. Christmas is a time of giving gifts to show love for others.

CHRISTMAS IS... CHRISTMAS DINNER.

There may be special foods and candies.

Often families and friends get together for a Christmas feast.

CHRISTMAS IS...CHRISTMAS CAROLS

Joy to the world! The Lord is come!

Peace on earth and mercy mild...

While mortals sleep, the angels keep their watch of wondrous love.

AND PRAYER, TOO.

On Christmas Eve and Christmas Day, many people go to church to hear the story of the Christ child's birth. They pray for good throughout the world.

CHRISTMAS IS...
PEACE, LOVE, AND JOY.